**Author**

*Tasha Ginn, M.Ed.*



**Editor**
Janet Cain, M.Ed.

**Managing Editor**
Ina Massler Levin, M.A.

**Editor-in-Chief**
Sharon Coan, M.S. Ed.

**Cover Artist**
Brenda DiAntonis

**Art Manager**
Kevin Barnes

**Art Director**
CJae Froshay

**Imaging**
James Edward Grace
Rosa C. See

**Product Manager**
Phil Garcia

**Publisher**
Mary D. Smith, M.S. Ed.

***Teacher Created Resources, Inc.***
6421 Industry Way
Westminster, CA 92683
www.teachercreated.com
**ISBN 13: 978-0-7439-3285-1**



Reprinted, 2007
Made in U.S.A.

# Table of Contents



 

# Introduction

All teachers want to stimulate an interest in reading in each student. However, oftentimes the pleasure of reading a novel, as well as the creative and critical thinking that may be sparked by the story, is stifled through activities such as report writing and test taking.

*Novel Assessments for Novels* is designed to provide you with creative assessment options. These assessments measure students' knowledge of a novel, while allowing students to explore the novel through multiple intelligences.

To promote the use of the multiple intelligences, encourage students to pursue unique approaches to the different assessments. Several of the assessments give an extension activity to further promote creativity and to access a variety of learning styles.

These assessments are best used after the completion of a novel. However, they can also be used at any point you feel that it is appropriate to assess students' understanding of a novel while it is being read.

You may wish to allow students to choose which assessment they want to complete after a class study of a novel. These assessments can also be used with novels that students have selected to read outside of class.

Many of the assessments in this book include a class presentation. This allows the entire class to learn from the presentations, thus helping students embrace their different learning styles.

This book provides a sample for each type of assessment to show how to complete the assignment. Each sample includes a scoring rubric. If you prefer to create your own rubric, a blank template is provided on page 79. Review the rubric while introducing the assignment so students know what is expected of them.

Each assessment activity will answer the following questions:

What does the activity assess?

- Language arts objectives
- Multiple intelligence(s)

What is the assessment activity?

- Description of the assessment activity
- Sample product

What do students need to complete the assessment activity?

- Student assignment/planning sheet
- Materials

How do I grade the assessment activity?

- Scoring rubric

# Multiple Intelligences

## Multiple Intelligences within Novel Assessments for Novels

The following chart shows which intelligences are tapped by each of the assessment activities in this book.

| | Intelligences | | | | | | |
|---|---|---|---|---|---|---|---|
| **Assessment Activity** | Linguistic | Logical | Spatial | Kinesthetic | Musical | Interpersonal | Intrapersonal |
| Talk Show | x | x | | | | x | |
| Tour Through a Novel's City or Town | x | | | x | x | | |
| Analysis of Character Development | x | | x | | | | |
| ABCs | x | | x | | | | |
| Character Predictions | x | x | | | | x | |
| Character Party | x | | | x | | x | |
| Role Playing | x | | | x | | | |
| Campaign | x | | | | | | x |
| Newspaper Article | x | | | | | | |
| Mock Trial | x | | | | | x | |
| Theme Quilt | x | | | x | | x | |
| Obituary | x | | | | | | |
| Children's Book | x | | | | | | |
| Advertisement | x | | | | | | |
| Mock Writer's Style | x | | | | | | |

## Multiple Intelligences

The seven multiple intelligences offer a holistic means to measure student learning. It allows students to use their preferred mode of learning in order to show the understanding they have gained from reading a novel.

- Linguistic Intelligence: the ability to use words effectively either through writing or verbally
- Logical Intelligence: the ability to view information in a logical sense; possibly able to learn information through characterization
- Spatial Intelligence: the ability to organize and present the information based on perceptions of the world
- Kinesthetic Intelligence: the ability to use the body to express ideas
- Musical Intelligence: the ability to identify and explain the elements of music
- Interpersonal Intelligence: the ability to identify the mood, feelings, and/or personality of an individual based on his/her gestures, voice, expressions, etc.
- Intrapersonal Intelligence: a strong sense of self and strengths; the ability to apply this self-awareness to the understanding of new material

# Talk Show

What does the activity assess?

- Language Arts Objectives
  - ❑ Analyze character development
  - ❑ Draw conclusions about story elements
- Multiple Intelligences
  - ❑ Linguistic
  - ❑ Logical
  - ❑ Interpersonal

What is the assessment activity?

This assessment allows students to use their communication skills as a means to discuss important topics from the novel being studied. The purpose is to explore how the important issues in the novel are not only relevant to the lives of the characters but also to the lives of the readers. Have students present a short mock television talk show. Encourage students to work cooperatively with a group to complete this assessment. Each group member will serve as a character from the novel. The talk show should be planned and rehearsed prior to the day of the performance.

During the presentation, students should express to the audience the significance of their topic. They should do this by incorporating quotes from the characters in the book. They can also do this by making inferences about the characters' feelings that were stated or implied in the story. Additionally, have students predict what might have happened to the characters beyond the ending that was provided in the book.

What do students need to complete the assessment activity?

- Student Assignment Sheet (page 6)
- Student Planning Sheet (pages 7 and 8)
- Sample Assessment (page 9)
- Scoring Rubric (page 10)
- Tables and chairs for the presentation

How do I grade the assessment activity?

As students are presenting the talk show based on an issue presented in the novel, use the scoring rubric (page 10) to evaluate the presentation. Consider all aspects of the talk show while deciding how students have met the expectations in each part of the rubric.

Name(s): ______________________________ Date: ____________

______________________________

# Student Assignment Sheet

You will write the script and hold a talk show based on the novel entitled

______________________________________________

as your final assessment. The topic of your talk show should stem from the important issues that are addressed in the novel. You are expected to have a talk show that causes your audience to think about those issues. To complete this assignment, you must work cooperatively with a group. The class will serve as your audience. One student should take on the role as the host or hostess of the show. The other group members should be different characters from the novel. Your group should write and plan the script prior to the day you present your talk show. Use the Student Planning Sheet and the Sample Assessment to help you prepare your presentation.

Please read and follow the guidelines below very carefully. The presentation of your talk show should include the following:

- A minimum of ten questions asked by the host/hostess
- Correct portrayal of the novel's characters
- Explanation of why the topics presented are significant in the novel

Your grade will be based on the Scoring Rubric. Please take time to review the rubric before creating and presenting your talk show.

 

Name(s): ______________________________ Date: ______________

______________________________

# Student Planning Sheet

Use this page and page 8 to plan your group's Talk Show presentation.

Title of novel: ______________________________

**Talk Show Characters**

| Name of Character | Basic Personality Traits |
| --- | --- |
| | |
| | |
| | |
| | |
| | |
| | |
| | |
| | |

Talk Show

Talk Show

# Student Planning Sheet *(cont.)*

**Talk Show Questions and Answers**

| | |
|---|---|
| **Host** (Introduction) | |
| **Host** (Question 1) | |
| **Character Name:** | |
| **Host** (Question 2) | |
| **Character Name:** | |
| **Host** (Question 3) | |
| **Character Name:** | |
| **Host** (Question 4) | |
| **Character Name:** | |
| **Host** (Question 5) | |
| **Character Name:** | |
| **Host** (Question 6) | |
| **Character Name:** | |
| **Host** (Question 7) | |
| **Character Name:** | |
| **Host** (Question 8) | |
| **Character Name:** | |
| **Host** (Question 9) | |
| **Character Name:** | |
| **Host** (Question 10) | |
| **Character Name:** | |

# Sample Assessment

(Excerpt from a Talk Show script based on *Mick Harte Was Here*)

**Host:** We are here today to discuss bike safety; more specifically, the need to wear helmets while riding a bicycle. A fun ride around the block can result in a fatal accident without a helmet. This is a fact that Mick Harte's family knows all too well. Today we will speak to his family about what they have endured. We will begin with Mick's parents, Mr. and Mrs. Harte.

**Mrs. Harte:** Thank you for having us here today to share our story.

**Host:** Thank you for coming. What happened to help your family realize the importance of bike safety?

**Mr. Harte:** I don't know where to begin. This is going to be harder than I thought.

**Host:** Take your time.

**Mrs. Harte:** It has been a devastating time for our family.

**Mr. Harte:** Yes, but we must share our story in hopes that no other family has to go through this. One evening, after school, our son Mick was riding his bike to a friend's house. He was not wearing a helmet. Why didn't I make him wear it?

**Mrs. Harte:** Remember, this is time for healing, not placing blame.

**Host:** What happened on the way to the friend's house?

**Mr. Harte:** Mick was hit by a car that evening. He died. In the accident, he suffered severe head injuries.

**Host:** Would a helmet really have made a difference in saving his life?

**Mrs. Harte:** Yes, according to the doctors, it would have. They say that an inch of Styrofoam alone would have made a difference between his living and dying. This is why we are here today, to share this information with the audience. One inch of Styrofoam would have made a difference. Mick was only in middle school — much too young to die.

**Host:** Thank you for sharing your story. Ladies and gentlemen, we must make sure our children wear helmets. As you can see from the Hartes' story, it can mean life or death. Now I would like to bring out Mick's sister, Phoebe.

**Host:** Hello, Phoebe. Welcome to the show.

**Phoebe:** Thanks for having me.

**Host:** What do you want to tell the audience about bike safety and your brother?

**Phoebe:** My brother didn't wear a helmet because he thought it made him look stupid. I would do anything to bring him back. It took almost a year for me to deal with his death. It's been really hard. What keeps me going are my memories of Mick. I know he was here and a part of my life, and no one can take that away from me.

Name(s): ______________________ Date: ____________

______________________

# Scoring Rubric

Title of novel: ______________________

| Criteria | Possible Number of Points | Score |
|---|---|---|
| Group works cooperatively and productively | 10 | |
| Presentation addresses an important topic from the novel | 10 | |
| Presentation sticks to the topic throughout | 10 | |
| Presentation is realistic and is formatted like a talk show | 10 | |
| Presentation is creative, interesting, and meaningful | 10 | |
| Presentation includes accurate information and relevant examples from the novel | 10 | |
| Presentation is well organized and easy to follow | 10 | |
| Presentation content flows smoothly | 10 | |
| Characterization is consistent with the novel in both spoken responses and mannerisms | 10 | |
| Presenters speak loudly and clearly, unless characterization dictates otherwise | 10 | |
| **Total Points** | 100 | |

**Teacher's Comments:**

 

# Tour Through a Novel's City or Town



What does the activity assess?

- Language Arts Objectives
  - ❑ Practice speaking skills
  - ❑ Improve reading comprehension
  - ❑ Analyze setting
  - ❑ Make connections between plot and setting
- Multiple Intelligences
  - ❑ Linguistic
  - ❑ Kinesthetic
  - ❑ Musical

What is the assessment activity?

This assessment allows students to creatively retell the story of a novel using the setting as a guide. Students may either do this assessment individually or with a group.

Students are expected to pretend that they are a tour guide that takes visitors around a city or town that is the main setting of the novel. If they choose to do this activity with a group, the other group members should pretend to be characters in the story that visitors would meet as they take the tour.

Students should address the importance of the setting and the significance of each location that is a point of interest during the tour.

Encourage students to dress in costumes and use props that reflect the novel's setting (place and time) and plot (events). Suggest to students that they use background music to help set the scene. Students may wish to create art work on butcher paper or poster board to enhance the visual effect for the audience.

What do students need to complete the assessment activity?

- Student Assignment Sheet (page 12)
- Student Planning Sheet (page 13)
- Sample Assessment (page 14)
- Scoring Rubric (page 15)
- Butcher paper or poster board
- Markers or paint
- Music (optional)
- Costumes
- Props

How do I grade the assessment activity?

This assessment is an excellent tool for evaluating the successful mastery of a variety of skills. Students will have as much fun creating the tour, as you will have grading it. Use the Scoring Rubric (page 15) as a guide for judging the quality of this assessment.

Name: ______________________________ Date: ______________

# Student Assignment Sheet

As your final assessment, you will serve as tour conductor for the settings of the novel entitled ______________________________.

You may choose to complete the assessment individually or with a group. Use the Student Planning Sheet and the Sample Assessment to help you prepare your tour.

Please read and follow the guidelines below very carefully. Your tour should include the following:

- A minimum of five different tour stops that are points of interest from the novel
- Description of an important event from the novel that occurred at each of the tour stops
- Artwork, music, props, and/or costumes to help recreate the scene

If you are completing this assessment with a group, your tour should also include the following:

- Group members playing the main characters from the novel
- Interaction between the guide and the characters as the tour takes place

Your grade will be based on the Scoring Rubric. Please take time to review the rubric before creating and presenting your tour.

Name(s): ______________________________ Date: ______________

______________________________

# Student Planning Sheet

When planning your tour, use this sheet to record relevant information from the novel. Then use the completed form to present your tour.

Title of novel: ______________________________

| Location of Tour Stop | Event from Novel | Audio/Visual Props (Examples: artwork, music, costumes, props) | Character(s) Involved |
|---|---|---|---|
| | | | |
| | | | |
| | | | |
| | | | |
| | | | |
| | | | |
| | | | |
| | | | |
| | | | |

# Sample Assessment

(Excerpt from a tour based on *Somewhere in the Darkness*)

**Note:** This group of students included a painting on butcher paper for each stop on the tour. Students who played the guide pretended to be driving a tour bus. Each time the tour guide pretended to stop the bus, another student would hold up the appropriate painting for the background.

**Visual:** Picture of a small apartment building in New York

**Tour Guide:** Good afternoon. I want to welcome you to a tour through the journey Jimmy took with his father, Crab. We must begin here, in New York. This is the small apartment building, the only home Jimmy ever knew. Jimmy lived with a lady he called Mama Jean. It was at the doorway of this apartment that Jimmy met his father, Crab, for the first time. Crab planned to move Jimmy and himself to Chicago.

**Visual:** Cleveland, Ohio

**Tour Guide:** Crab and Jimmy drove to Chicago. On their way, they passed through Cleveland. It was here that Jimmy found out that Crab had been in jail for killing someone.

**Visual:** Small, dirty room in a boarding house

**Tour Guide:** Crab and Jimmy's road trip finally led them to their original destination of Chicago. In Chicago, Crab and Jimmy shared this small, dirty room in a boarding house. As you can see, this room only holds two single beds and a chest of drawers.

**Visual:** Memphis, Tennessee

**Tour Guide:** While on their trip, Crab and Jimmy briefly stopped in Memphis, Tennessee. Jimmy heard stories about his father's childhood. Unfortunately, this included the story of Jimmy's grandfather.

**Visual:** Arkansas

**Tour Guide**: Crab decided to make Arkansas the next stop. Arkansas becomes a crucial place for Jimmy and Crab. Jimmy spoke to Mama Jean on the phone for the first time since he left New York. He fought back his own tears when he heard her cry.

**Visual:** Prison

**Tour Guide:** Crab finally told Jimmy that he escaped from prison. He explained that he wanted Jimmy to know he was innocent, and the only way he could do that was to find Rydell. But that never happened because Crab died.

 

Name(s): ______________________________ Date: ______________

______________________________

# Scoring Rubric

Title of novel: ______________________________

| Criteria | Possible Number of Points | Score |
|---|---|---|
| Tour includes a minimum of five stops | 10 | |
| Guide tells a relevant event from the novel for each stop on the tour | 10 | |
| Presentation is realistic and is formatted like a tour | 10 | |
| Tour is creative and interesting | 10 | |
| Tour includes accurate information from the novel | 10 | |
| Tour information is well organized and easy to follow | 10 | |
| Tour information flows smoothly | 10 | |
| Tour includes information about main characters from the novel or, if done with a group, incorporates main characters from the novel into the tour | 10 | |
| Scenes are effectively recreated using audio/visual props (artwork, music, costumes, props, etc.) | 10 | |
| Tour guide speaks loudly and clearly | 10 | |
| **Total Points** | 100 | |

**Teacher's Comments:**

# Analysis of Character Development

What does the activity assess?

- Language Arts Objectives
  - ❑ Understand elements of character development
  - ❑ Draw conclusions about story elements
  - ❑ Analyze setting
  - ❑ Make connections between plot and setting
- Multiple Intelligences
  - ❑ Linguistic
  - ❑ Spatial

What is the assessment activity?

This assessment is presented in a chart format and allows students to analyze how a character's decisions affect a personality change from the beginning to the end of the novel.

Students are expected to identify a minimum of five events that helped shape the character into the person he or she is by the end of the book. The chart allows students to analyze the events that cause a character to change. The chart can be presented on poster board or using computer software.

What do students need to complete the assessment activity?

- Student Assignment Sheet (page 17)
- Student Planning Sheet (page 18)
- Sample Assessment (page 19)
- Scoring Rubric (page 20)
- Poster board and markers or computer software that can be used to make a chart

How do I grade the assessment activity?

Evaluate the student's ability to analyze characters and make connections within the text using the Scoring Rubric (page 20).

 

Name: ______________________________ Date: ______________

# Student Assignment Sheet



For this assessment, you will create a chart as you analyze a character's development from the novel entitled ______________________.

You may complete the assignment on a piece of poster board or using computer software. Use the Student Planning Sheet and the Sample Assessment to help you analyze a character in the novel.

Please read and follow the guidelines below very carefully. Your chart should include the following:

- Identification and focus on just one character from the novel
- A minimum of five traits that can be used to describe the chosen character
- Key decisions or events from the novel that provide evidence of each character trait
- Explanation and analysis of how the decision or event helped define the character and show change over the time of the novel

Your grade will be based on the Scoring Rubric. Please take time to review the rubric before completing the chart for this assessment.

Name: ____________________ Date: __________

# Student Planning Sheet

As you read the novel, use this sheet to record information about a character. Include information about key decisions and/or events that help shape the character into the person he or she is.

Title of novel: ____________________

Name of character being analyzed: ____________________

| Character Trait | Key Decision and/or Event that Shows the Character Trait | What This Tells the Reader About the Character |
|---|---|---|
| | | |
| | | |
| | | |
| | | |
| | | |
| | | |
| | | |
| | | |

 

# Sample Assessment

(Excerpt from a character analysis chart based on *Crash*)

Title of novel: *Crash*

Name of character being analyzed: Crash

| Character Trait | Key Decision and/or Event that Shows the Character Trait | What This Tells the Reader About the Character |
|---|---|---|
| Cruelty | Putting mustard in Penn's shoes | Crash is probably attempting to make up for lack of attention at home by following along with Mike's idea for this prank. Crash also gets easily upset at people, while Penn remains happy despite what others do to him. This increases the irony of Penn and Crash becoming best friends by the end of the book. |
| Loving | Reading of the essay about Scooter | This is the climax of the change in Crash. He begins to focus on the many great things Scooter has accomplished for the family. Crash realizes the importance of family. The reading of Penn's essay serves to enhance this feeling. Crash now has a reason to move from his pettiness to values that actually hold meaning. This also gives him a reason to let Penn win the race. Penn is doing it for his great grandfather; Crash finally understands the meaning of this. |
| Stubborn | Refusing to leave the football field when the coach was trying to put in the second-string quarterback | Crash is again trying to show that he can do whatever he wants to do. He does not want to lose the attention he is currently getting from the crowd, so he refuses to do what the coach tells him. He definitely shows stubbornness when he refuses to leave even when the coach approaches the field. |
| Feeling incomplete and disappointed | Always looks for his parents at his football games | Although Crash is the star football player who gets a lot of praise from the fans, he does not feel complete. He is disappointed because he never sees his parents cheering him on in the stands. Since he tries to be so tough, he does not tell anyone that it bothers him. However, it is obvious from his actions that he cares about his parents' lack of support. |

Name(s): ______________________________ Date: ______________

# Scoring Rubric

Title of novel: ______________________________

Name of character being analyzed: ______________________________

| Criteria | Possible Number of Points | Score |
|---|---|---|
| Chart names the character to be analyzed | 10 | |
| Chart lists a minimum of five character traits | 10 | |
| Chart includes key decisions/events that provide evidence of each character trait | 10 | |
| Information from the novel that is used as supporting evidence is accurate | 10 | |
| Chart includes a logical explanation and analysis of how the decision or event helped shape the character | 10 | |
| Analysis shows how the character changes over the time of the novel | 10 | |
| Information in the chart is well organized and easy to follow | 10 | |
| Information in the chart is neat and easy to read | 10 | |
| Information in the chart has few spelling, capitalization, or punctuation errors | 10 | |
| Information in the chart has few grammatical errors | 10 | |
| **Total Points** | 100 | |

**Teacher's Comments:**

 

# ABCs



What does the activity assess?

- Language Arts Objectives
  - ❑ Understand elements of character development
  - ❑ Improve reading comprehension
- Multiple Intelligences
  - ❑ Linguistic
  - ❑ Spatial

What is the assessment activity?

This assessment allows students to summarize important information from the novel in a creative manner. Have students use the planning sheet (page 23) to identify important people, places, and events from the novel that start with each letter of the alphabet. Then tell students to transfer the information from the planning sheet to a piece of poster board.

Ask students to complete the poster board and then present either a portion or all of the ABCs.

This activity serves as a great review for a traditional assessment. Additionally, it can be used to give students practice with vocabulary words.

What do students need to complete the assessment activity?

- Student Assignment Sheet (page 22)
- Student Planning Sheet (page 23)
- Sample Assessment (page 24)
- Scoring Rubric (page 25)
- Poster board
- Markers

How do I grade the assessment activity?

Evaluate the student's ability to summarize important information from the novel using the Scoring Rubric (page 25).

Name(s): ______________________________ Date: ______________

______________________________

# Student Assignment Sheet

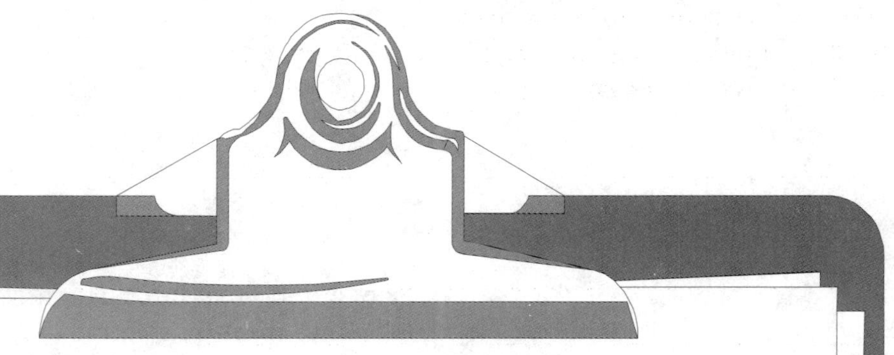

As your final assessment, you will create an ABC list of important information from the novel entitled

______________________________________________.

Your ABC list should be presented on a piece of poster board. For each letter of the alphabet, be sure to write a word, phrase, or sentence that tells about important people, places, and events from the novel. You may complete this assessment individually or with a group. Use the Student Planning Sheet and the Sample Assessment to help you prepare your ABC list.

Please read and follow the guidelines below very carefully. Your ABC list should include the following:

- Twenty-six phrases or sentences that tell about important people, places, and events from the novel
- Phrases and sentences that start with the corresponding letter
- An emphasis on important elements from the novel
- A list that works together as a summary of the novel

Your grade will be based on the Scoring Rubric. Please take time to review the rubric before completing the ABC list.

 

Name: ______________________ Date: ____________

# Student Planning Sheet

Use the following lines to brainstorm possible words, phrases, or sentences for each letter of the alphabet. Be sure to focus on important people, places, and events in the novel. Then use this sheet to create an original list on a piece of poster board.

A ______________________

B ______________________

C ______________________

D ______________________

E ______________________

F ______________________

G ______________________

H ______________________

I ______________________

J ______________________

K ______________________

L ______________________

M ______________________

N ______________________

O ______________________

P ______________________

Q ______________________

R ______________________

S ______________________

T ______________________

U ______________________

V ______________________

W ______________________

X ______________________

Y ______________________

Z ______________________

# Sample Assessment

(ABCs based on *Joey Pigza Swallowed the Key*)

**A** is for the apple slices Joey is sent to the bus to eat

**B** is for the bandages Joey loves to wear

**C** is for Charlie

**D** is for the dog (Chihuahua) Joey wants

**E** is for the eagerness Joey always feels

**F** is for the flies Joey thinks he will find in the pie

**G** is for Joey's grandma

**H** is for the happiness Joey feels when he is good

**I** is for the innocence that Joey feels when he gets in trouble

**J** is for Joey

**K** is for the key Joey swallows

**L** is for the love Joey's mother feels for him

**M** is for the molasses shoofly pie

**N** is for Nurse Holyfield who always listens to Joey

**O** is for the out of control actions that Joey sometimes has

**P** is for the pumpkin patches, pills, and puppy

**Q** is for questions Joey's teacher has about his behavior

**R** is for the refrigerator Joey's grandma tries to put him in

**S** is for the scissors Joey stabs Maria with

**T** is for terrible, which is how everyone describes Joey's behavior

**U** is for the unpredictable behavior that Joey sometimes has

**V** is for the victory Joey feels when he finally learns to control his behavior

**W** is for wired, the word people use to describe Joey

**X** is for the x-ray type pictures that are taken of Joey's brain

**Y** is for the yearning Joey feels to be good

**Z** is for zest for life and fun that Joey has

 

Name: ______________________ Date: ______________

# Scoring Rubric

ABCs

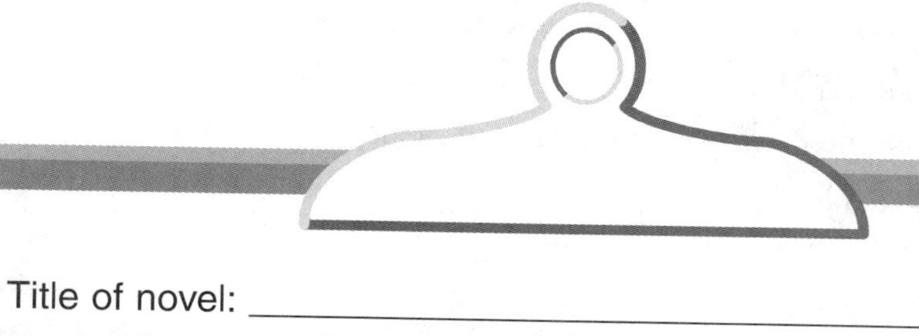

Title of novel: ______________________________

| Criteria | Possible Number of Points | Score |
| --- | --- | --- |
| List includes 26 people, places, and/or events from the novel | 10 | |
| List includes only important people, places, and/or events | 10 | |
| Information from the novel corresponds with each letter on the list | 10 | |
| List is creative, interesting, and meaningful | 10 | |
| List includes accurate information from the novel | 10 | |
| List is well organized and easy to understand | 10 | |
| List is neat and easy to read | 10 | |
| List has few spelling, capitalization, and punctuation errors | 10 | |
| List has few grammatical errors | 10 | |
| Presenters speak loudly and clearly | 10 | |
| **Total Points** | 100 | |

**Teacher's Comments:**

# Character Predictions

What does the activity assess?

- Language Arts Objectives
  - ❑ Reflect on what has been read
  - ❑ Formulate ideas and responses to texts
  - ❑ Make inferences and draw conclusions about story elements
  - ❑ Understand elements of character development
- Multiple Intelligences
  - ❑ Linguistic
  - ❑ Logical
  - ❑ Interpersonal

What is the assessment activity?

This assessment allows students to explain a character's motives that are implied in the novel.

Have students pretend that they are a character from the novel. Tell them to use the events in the novel to make educated predictions about the unrevealed thoughts of the character. Remind students that their predictions should be expressed in first person narrative as if they are actually that character. Point out that the other students should feel as if they are meeting the character.

Expect students to address the important events that have an impact on who the character is and why he or she makes certain decisions.

Encourage students to dress in a costume that reflects the personality and behavior of the character. Students may also wish to use props. Then invite students to present a monologue as if the character were speaking.

What do students need to complete the assessment activity?

- Student Assignment Sheet (page 27)
- Sample Assessment (page 28)
- Scoring Rubric (page 29)
- Notebook paper for planning the monologue
- Costume
- Props (optional)

How do I grade the assessment activity?

Evaluate the student's ability to make predictions about a character using the Scoring Rubric (page 29).

Name: ______________________ Date: ______________

# Student Assignment Sheet



As your final assessment, you will serve as the conscience of a character from the novel entitled ______________________.

This means you will pretend to be the character and tell your innermost thoughts and feelings. Your presentation will be in a monologue format. Use the Sample Assessment to help you prepare your monologue.

Please read and follow the guidelines below very carefully. Use a blank piece of paper to plan your monologue. Your monologue should include the following:

- The name of the character you are pretending to be
- Reasonable predictions that explain why the character acts a certain way
- Statements that reveal the character's innermost thoughts and feelings
- Details from the story that support your character's words

Your grade will be based on the Scoring Rubric. Please take time to review the rubric before completing your monologue.

# Sample Assessment

(Character Predictions monologue based on *The Chocolate War*)

**Note:** The props consisted of a photograph that showed the presenter's mother and father, as well as a chocolate bar.

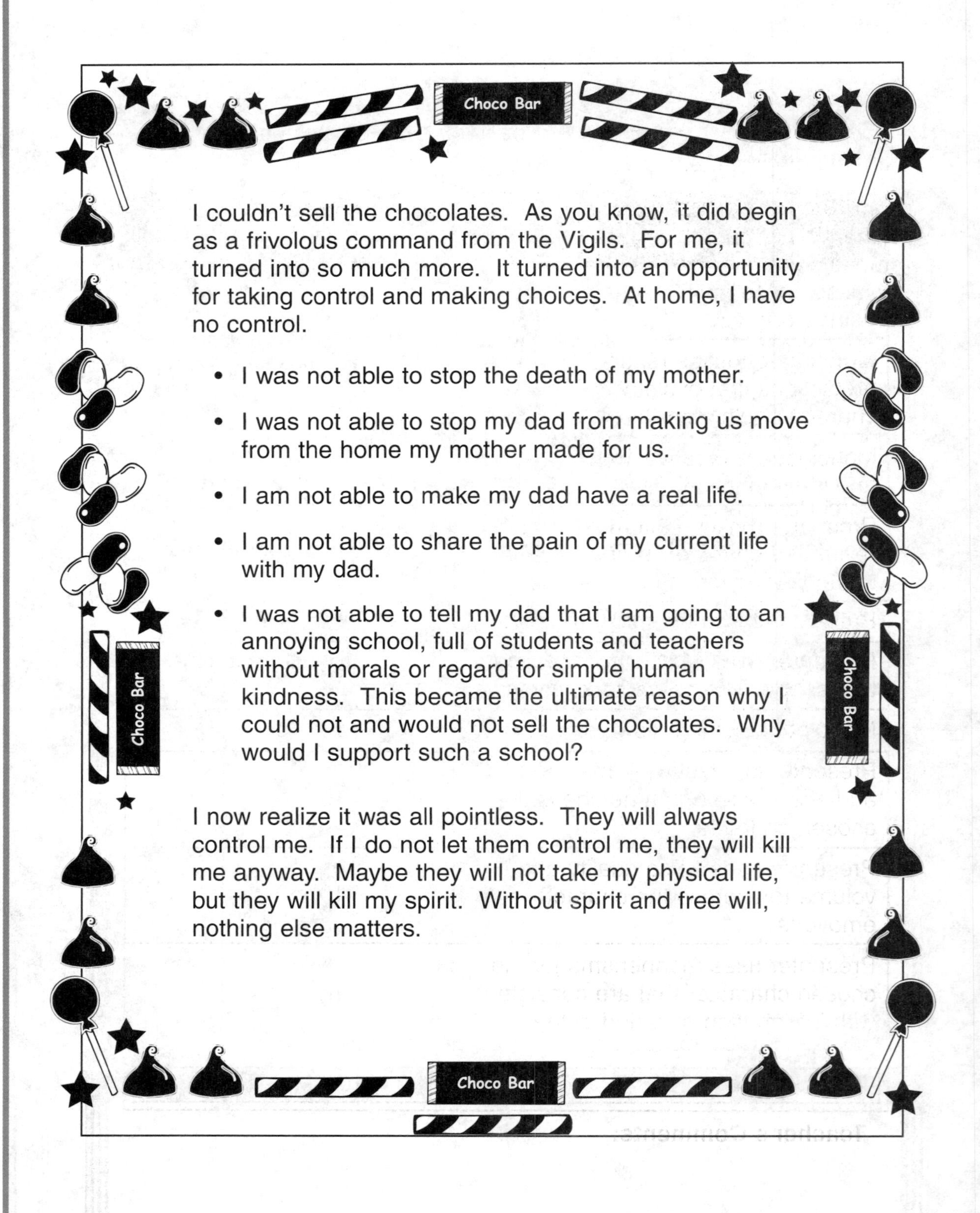


I couldn't sell the chocolates. As you know, it did begin as a frivolous command from the Vigils. For me, it turned into so much more. It turned into an opportunity for taking control and making choices. At home, I have no control.

- I was not able to stop the death of my mother.
- I was not able to stop my dad from making us move from the home my mother made for us.
- I am not able to make my dad have a real life.
- I am not able to share the pain of my current life with my dad.
- I was not able to tell my dad that I am going to an annoying school, full of students and teachers without morals or regard for simple human kindness. This became the ultimate reason why I could not and would not sell the chocolates. Why would I support such a school?

I now realize it was all pointless. They will always control me. If I do not let them control me, they will kill me anyway. Maybe they will not take my physical life, but they will kill my spirit. Without spirit and free will, nothing else matters.

 

Name: ______________________________ Date: ______________

# Scoring Rubric

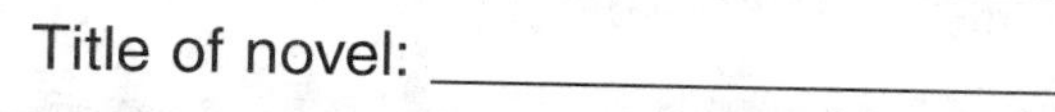

Title of novel: ______________________________

| Criteria | Possible Number of Points | Score |
|---|---|---|
| Presenter tells which character is being portrayed | 10 | |
| Monologue makes reasonable predictions that explain why the character acts a certain way | 10 | |
| Monologue is creative, well organized, and easy to follow | 10 | |
| Presenter makes statements that reveal the character's innermost thoughts and feelings | 10 | |
| Presenter sticks to topic throughout | 10 | |
| Presenter uses details from the story that support the character's words | 10 | |
| Monologue content flows smoothly | 10 | |
| Presenter is effective in making the audience believe that he/she is the chosen character | 10 | |
| Presenter uses voice quality and volume to express the character's emotions | 10 | |
| Presenter uses mannerisms for the chosen character that are consistent with information provided in the novel | 10 | |
| **Total Points** | 100 | |

**Teacher's Comments:**

# Character Party

What does the activity assess?

- Language Arts Objectives
  - Analyze characters
  - Recognize story plot
  - Understand relationships among characters in a text
  - Recognize point of view
  - Improve reading comprehension
- Multiple Intelligences
  - Linguistic
  - Kinesthetic
  - Interpersonal

What is the assessment activity?

Use strips of paper to write the names of the different characters in the novel. Be sure you have one strip for each student, since each member of the class will need to be assigned one of the novel's characters. With a large class, you may need each character's name to appear on more than one strip. Fold the strips and then place them in a container. Give students their assignments the day of the party by inviting them to draw a strip of paper out of the container. Keep a record of which students are assigned to each character. Tell students to keep their character assignments a secret.

Expect students to know everything their character in the story knows about the plot of the novel. They must pretend that they do not know any information that was not revealed to their particular character in the course of the novel. Ask students to mingle as if they are at a party and participate in conversations that simulate what the characters of the novel would discuss. Remind students not to reveal which character they are playing. During the party, encourage students to use conversation and mannerism clues to figure out which character each student is playing.

Block scheduling lends itself well to this assignment. However, the assignment can also be completed in one or two traditional class periods.

To help make the party more festive, you may wish to bring snacks for students or invite them to bring their own.

Serve as a facilitator during the party to make sure that all students stay on task and to assess students based on the rubric.

What do students need to complete the assessment activity?

- Student Assignment Sheet (pages 31 and 32)
- Sample Assessment (page 33)
- Scoring Rubric (page 34)
- Snacks (optional)

How do I grade the assessment activity?

Evaluate the student's ability to accurately portray a character from a novel using the Scoring Rubric (page 34).

 

Name: ____________________ Date: ____________

# Student Assignment Sheet



Your final assessment of the novel

______________________________

will take place during a class party. Use the Sample Assessment to help you prepare for your party.

Please read and follow the guidelines below very carefully. On the day of the party, you will be expected to:

- Have read the novel named above
- Have full knowledge of the plot, setting, and characters
- Use information from the novel to accurately portray an assigned character
- Converse with other students while pretending to be the assigned character
- Remain "in character" for the duration of the party
- Pay close attention to the words and mannerisms of other students
- Evaluate the words and mannerisms of other students in order to guess which characters they are portraying
- Identify as many characters as possible, keeping in mind that more than one student might be assigned to play the same character
- Complete the "Who's Who?" chart (page 32)

Your grade will be based on the Scoring Rubric. Please take time to review the rubric before participating in the Character Party.

Name: ______________________________ Date: ______________

# Student Assignment Sheet *(cont.)*

Please make a list of all the students in your class. As you participate in the Character Party, pay close attention to the words and mannerisms of the other students. Use this page to guess which character each of your classmates is portraying.

## Who's Who?

| Name of Student | Name of Character Being Portrayed |
|---|---|
| 1. | 1. |
| 2. | 2. |
| 3. | 3. |
| 4. | 4. |
| 5. | 5. |
| 6. | 6. |
| 7. | 7. |
| 8. | 8. |
| 9. | 9. |
| 10. | 10. |
| 11. | 11. |
| 12. | 12. |
| 13. | 13. |
| 14. | 14. |
| 15. | 15. |
| 16. | 16. |
| 17. | 17. |
| 18. | 18. |
| 19. | 19. |
| 20. | 20. |
| 21. | 21. |
| 22. | 22. |
| 23. | 23. |
| 24. | 24. |
| 25. | 25. |
| 26. | 26. |
| 27. | 27. |
| 28. | 28. |
| 29. | 29. |
| 30. | 30. |

# Sample Assessment

(Excerpts from Character Party dialogues based on *To Kill a Mockingbird*)

**Dialogue 1**

"It is hard to enjoy this wonderful party while the Robinson family is at home worrying about Tom Robinson. But I know he will not be put in jail as long as my father, Atticus, is his lawyer."

"Your father is not that great of a lawyer to be able to prevent that guilty black man from going to jail."

"See he is great—that is why he is defending Tom even though many people say that he should not."

**Dialogue 2**

"I can't believe you allowed those children to, not only sit through the court session, but to sit in the colored section at that."

"The children had a right to see what was going on. I couldn't sit in the white section, so what choice did I have?"

"The children came home and wanted to know about the word 'nigger.' "

"I told you this would happen. That's why I'm here to help raise them and give them proper influence."

**Dialogue 3**

"I am defending Tom because I have to. Defending him is a part of me being a lawyer. This case will probably change my life more than any other case I will ever have to take to trial."

"Does that mean you think you can win the trial?"

"Probably not."

"Then why bother, and why work so hard?"

"Some things you have to do, even if you know you may not win."

Name: ______________________ Date: ____________

# Scoring Rubric

Title of novel: ______________________

| Criteria | Possible Number of Points | Score |
|---|---|---|
| Works cooperatively and politely during the party, unless characterization dictates otherwise | 10 | |
| Shows complete knowledge and understanding of the plot, setting, and characters | 10 | |
| Uses information from the novel to accurately portray an assigned character | 10 | |
| Converses with other students while pretending to be the assigned character | 10 | |
| Discussion is strictly limited to topics that the character in the story knows | 10 | |
| Role play is creative, interesting, and meaningful | 10 | |
| Remains "in character" for the duration of the party | 10 | |
| Pays close attention to the words and mannerisms of other students | 10 | |
| Uses logical deductions to identify as many characters as possible during the party | 10 | |
| Completes as much of the "Who's Who?" chart as possible | 10 | |
| **Total Points** | 100 | |

**Teacher's Comments:**

 

# Role Playing

What does the activity assess?

- Language Arts Objectives
  - ❑ Understand elements of character development
  - ❑ Make inferences and draw conclusions about story elements
- Language Arts Objectives
  - ❑ Linguistic
  - ❑ Kinesthetic

What is the assessment activity?

This assessment allows students to creatively present a scene from the novel. Students can work individually or with a group. Have students pretend that they are characters from the book. The role play should be planned and rehearsed prior to the day of the performance.

In the role play, have students address the importance of the scene and explain what it teaches the reader about the overall book.

Encourage students to dress in costumes and use props that reflect the novel's setting (place and time) and plot (events). Suggest to students that they use background music to help set the scene. Students may wish to create artwork on butcher paper or poster board to enhance the visual effects for the audience.

What do students need to complete the assessment activity?

- Student Assignment Sheet (page 36)
- Student Planning Sheet (page 37)
- Sample Assessment (page 38)
- Scoring Rubric (page 39)
- Butcher paper or poster board
- Markers or paint
- Costumes
- Props
- Music (optional)

How do I grade the assessment activity?

Evaluate the student's ability to role play using the Scoring Rubric (page 39).

Name(s): ______________________________ Date: ______________

______________________________

# Student Assignment Sheet

As your final assessment, you will present a scene from the novel entitled ______________________________________________.

You may choose to complete the assessment individually or with a group. Use the Student Planning Sheet and the Sample Assessment to help you prepare your role play.

Please read and follow the guidelines below very carefully. Your performance should:

- Be at least five minutes in length
- Have full knowledge of the plot, setting, and characters for the chosen scene
- Effectively recreate the scene using audio/visual props (artwork, music, costumes, props, etc.)
- Use information from the novel to accurately portray a character
- Use words and mannerisms to emulate both the personality and dialect of the character
- Remain "in character" for the duration of the scene
- Explain why the chosen scene is important

Your grade will be based on the Scoring Rubric. Please take time to review the rubric before planning and presenting the scene you have chosen.

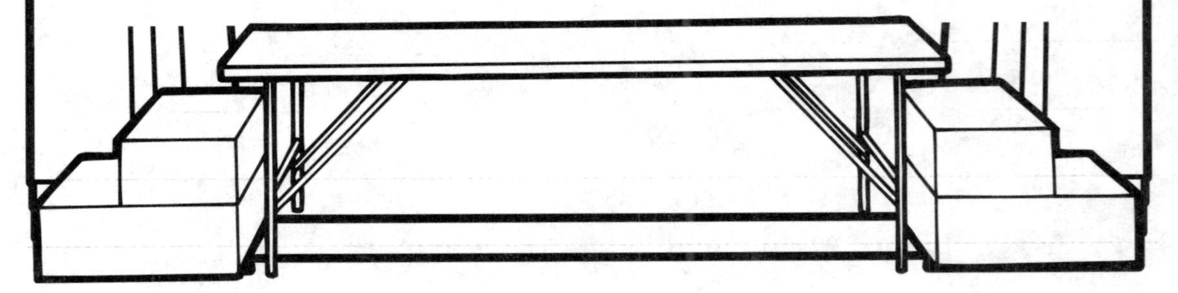

 

Name(s): ______________________________ Date: ______________

______________________________

# Student Planning Sheet

Title of novel: ________________________________________

Brief description of scene: ________________________________________

________________________________________

________________________________________

Use the chart below to plan your role-playing performance.

| Name of Character | Description of Costume | Information from Novel for Dialogue | Description of Props |
|---|---|---|---|
| | | | |
| | | | |
| | | | |
| | | | |
| | | | |

On a separate piece of paper, write the script for the dialogue using the information you have recorded in this chart.

Use the space below to explain why this scene is important.

________________________________________

________________________________________

________________________________________

________________________________________

________________________________________

________________________________________

Role Playing

# Sample Assessment

(Excerpt of dialogue based on *The Watsons Go to Birmingham—1963*)

**Note:** For the visual, students used butcher paper to paint a brown car covered with snow and ice. Two students are holding ice scrapers. One student plays the role of Kenny, while another plays the role of Byron.

**Kenny:** It is too cold for anyone to be outside. I cannot believe we have to scrape this ice.

**Byron:** Stop complaining. This gives you the opportunity to see me, your good-looking brother. I am still trying to figure out where I get my looks from.

**Kenny:** Whatever. I am going to start scraping. You better start because I am not going to do your half.

**Byron:** Awwww.

**Kenny:** Stop wasting time; start scraping!

**Byron:** I look too good to be out in this cold weather scraping ice. I don't know how I became part of this ugly family.

**Kenny:** Oh, we are ugly because we don't stop at every mirror to look at ourselves. Stop looking in that mirror and start scraping.

**Byron:** Does it really take two people to do this?

**Kenny:** Yes.

**Byron:** So why doesn't Dad come and help?

**Kenny:** Because he told us to do it, so you better get busy—fast.

**Byron:** (Kisses the car mirror and his lip gets stuck to it) Help!

**Kenny:** You won't get me with your tricks this time.

**Byron:** Really—I need help. Please.

**Kenny:** Oh, my goodness! Your lip is stuck to the mirror!

**Byron:** Help!

**Kenny**: I'll get Dad.

**Byron:** Hurry!

**Explanation of Importance**: This scene shows the relationship between the two brothers that is stressed throughout the book. Although Kenny is younger than Byron, he proves himself as more mature through several events. In this scene, Kenny goes outside and immediately begins the work he was instructed to do by his father, even though he does not want to do the task. However, Byron plays around and only wants to admire his good looks. When he kisses himself in the car's mirror, he gets stuck and Kenny has to run for help.

 

Name(s): ______________________ Date: ______________

______________________



# Scoring Rubric

Title of novel: ______________________

| Criteria | Possible Number of Points | Score |
|---|---|---|
| Role play presents an important scene from the novel | 10 | |
| Scene is effectively recreated using audio/visual props (artwork, music, costumes, props, etc.) | 10 | |
| Role play is at least five minutes in length | 10 | |
| Role play is creative, interesting, and meaningful | 10 | |
| Role play includes accurate information from the novel | 10 | |
| Role play is well organized and easy to follow | 10 | |
| Presenters remain "in character" for the duration of the role play | 10 | |
| Characterization is consistent with the novel in both words and mannerisms | 10 | |
| Presenters speak loudly and clearly, unless characterization dictates otherwise | 10 | |
| Presenters explain the importance of the scene | 10 | |
| **Total Points** | 100 | |

**Teacher's Comments:**

# Campaign

What does the activity assess?

- Language Arts Objectives
  - ❑ Establish and adjust purposes for reading
- Multiple Intelligences
  - ❑ Linguistic
  - ❑ Intrapersonal

What is the assessment activity?

This assessment should be used with a book that addresses a serious social issue. It gives students the opportunity to learn about things that are serious concerns for society as a whole, while encouraging them to help find answers/solutions to the problem. Students may either do this assessment individually or with a group.

Ask students to pretend that they are launching a community awareness campaign for the social issue that is presented in the novel.

Have students address the importance of the issue and explain the need for the campaign. Point out to students that they will need to do research about the topic to find out accurate information and valuable statistics that they can use in their campaign.

Ideally, students should try to fit the campaign in the actual setting and circumstances of the novel. The presentation should be structured as if students have stepped into the world of the novel.

What do students need to complete the assessment activity?

- Student Assignment Sheet (page 41)
- Student Planning Sheet (page 42)
- Sample Assessment (page 43)
- Scoring Rubric (page 44)
- Access to a library or a computer for research materials
- Notebook paper

How do I grade the assessment activity?

Use the Scoring Rubric (page 44) to evaluate students' abilities to create a campaign that includes factual information, is persuasive, and suggests a viable solution/answer to the problem.

 

Name(s): ______________________________ Date: ______________

______________________________

# Student Assignment Sheet

Title of novel: ____________________________________________



You will serve as a campaign manager for an important social issue presented in the novel entitled ______________________.

As the campaign manager, it is your job to increase community awareness about this issue and suggest a solution/answer to the problem. Your campaign will be your final assessment for this novel. You may choose to complete the assessment individually or with a group. Use the Student Planning Sheet and the Sample Assessment to help you prepare your campaign.

Please read and follow the guidelines below very carefully. Your campaign should include:

- Valuable information and statistics gathered from research
- Explanation of the connection to the novel
- Effective balance and transition into the setting of the novel
- The names of the characters that are involved with the issue in the novel
- At least three strategies for ways to increase awareness about the issue
- At least one viable solution/answer to the problem

Your grade will be based on the Scoring Rubric. Please take time to review the rubric before completing your campaign.

Name(s): ______________________________ Date: ______________

______________________________

# Student Planning Sheet

Title of novel: ______________________________

## Campaign Plan

| | |
|---|---|
| **Campaign Topic**<br>(What is the social issue presented in the novel?) | |
| **Campaign Strategies**<br>(How should you increase awareness about the social issue?) | |
| **Possible Solutions/Answers to Problem**<br>(What can people do to help solve the problem?) | |

## Supporting Research

| Source | Statistics or Other Factual Data for Campaign |
|---|---|
| | |
| | |
| | |

 

# Sample Assessment

(Excerpt from a campaign based on *Hang Tough, Paul Mather*)

**Note:** Three students play the roles of three characters from the book: Monk, Tip, and Abels. They put together a campaign to present to the student body of the school. The problem addressed by their campaign is leukemia. Their proposed solution to the problem is a fundraiser that earns money for leukemia research.

### Campaign Speech

As most of you know, Paul Mather, one of the students from our school, has leukemia. We feel it is important to help scientists find a cure for this disease so Paul can play baseball again; he is an amazing player. Here is our plan.

We will have a series of baseball games. We will have four league teams participating. The entrance fee to see each game will be a $5.00 donation. In addition, all money earned by the concessions stand will also be donated to leukemia research.

We have invited the local news stations to tape parts of the game and put it on the air so Paul can see how we are trying to help him. We hope the media coverage will also encourage people who cannot attend the game to send in donations.

We are calling this event "A Homerun for Paul." We hope it will become an annual event to help Paul and others who suffer from leukemia.

Name(s): ______________________________ Date: ______________

______________________________

# Scoring Rubric

Title of novel: ______________________________

| Criteria | Possible Number of Points | Score |
|---|---|---|
| Campaign addresses an important social issue | 10 | |
| Connection between the novel and campaign issue is obvious | 10 | |
| Information gathered from research is accurate and relevant | 10 | |
| Campaign sticks to the topic throughout | 10 | |
| Campaign is creative, interesting, meaningful, and persuasive | 10 | |
| Campaign is well organized and easy to follow | 10 | |
| Campaign has an effective balance and transition into the setting of the novel | 10 | |
| Campaign uses characters that are involved with the issue in the novel | 10 | |
| Campaign includes at least three strategies for ways to increase awareness about the issue | 10 | |
| Campaign suggests at least one viable solution/answer to the problem | 10 | |
| **Total Points** | 100 | |

**Teacher's Comments:**

 

# Newspaper Article

What does the activity assess?

- Language Arts Objectives
  - ❑ Summarize the novel
  - ❑ Improve reading comprehension
  - ❑ Review and analyze literature
- Multiple Intelligences
  - ❑ Linguistic

What is the assessment activity?

This is an assessment that allows students the opportunity to practice journalistic writing techniques while studying an important time period in history. The purpose is to identify areas of a novel that would be considered newsworthy events. Invite students to write a newspaper story that tells important events from the novel. Students can choose to either complete this assessment individually or with a group.

Tell students to inform the audience about the important events described in the book. Students should do this by incorporating quotes from characters and including relevant details. Overall, the news story should provide a summary of the major events described in the novel.

To extend this assessment, groups may wish to take the assignment further by creating a newspaper with several sections. The articles and advertisements included in the newspaper should represent the time period of the book and tell about important people, places, and events.

As an alternative, students may wish to create a television news show that tells about the important people, places, and events from the novel.

What do students need to complete the assessment activity?

- Student Assignment Sheet (page 46)
- Student Planning Sheet (page 47)
- Sample Assessment (page 48)
- Scoring Rubric (page 49)
- Access to a computer with word-processing software (optional)

How do I grade the assessment activity?

Use the Scoring Rubric (page 49) to evaluate students' abilities to write a newspaper article related to important events described in the novel.

Name(s): ______________________________ Date: ______________

______________________________

# Student Assignment Sheet

## EXTRA!!! NOVEL NEWS EXTRA!!!

As your final assessment, you will write a newspaper article for the novel entitled ______________________________.

Your newspaper should resemble the format of an actual newspaper article. You are expected to create one or more original newspaper articles that will help people who have never read the novel to understand and visualize the event(s) that you are choosing to report. You may complete this assessment individually or with a group. If you choose to do the assessment with a group, each member should complete his or her own article. Then work together to create a newspaper with the articles. Use the Student Planning Sheet and the Sample Assessment to help you prepare your newspaper.

Please read and follow the guidelines below very carefully. Your newspaper article should include the following:

- A specific event or series of events described in the novel
- Names of the characters involved in the event(s)
- Relevant quotes from the characters
- An explanation of why the event or series of events is important to the story

Your grade will be based on the Scoring Rubric. Please take time to review the rubric before writing your newspaper article.

 

Name(s): ______________________________ Date: ______________

______________________________

# Student Planning Sheet

Newspaper Article

## Content

| | |
|---|---|
| Subject of Article | |
| Connection to Novel | |
| Characters | |
| Setting | |
| Important Quotes | |

## Organization

| | |
|---|---|
| Paragraph One | |
| Paragraph Two | |
| Paragraph Three | |
| Paragraph Four | |
| Paragraph Five | |
| Paragraph Six | |

Newspaper Article

# Sample Assessment

(Newspaper Article based on *Number the Stars*)


## Star of David

VOLUME 1, ISSUE 1
April 1943


### Young Girl Risks Her Life to Deliver Bread

By Carla Goldstein

**INSIDE THIS ISSUE:**



Without thinking about the danger, Annemarie volunteered to take the package to her Uncle Henrik. As she and her mother packed the lunch basket as a cover, Annemarie's mother warned her of the risk. But only enough to understand the danger, not enough to let her know just how much danger.

As Annmarie walked through the woods, she ignored the noises that she kept hearing. However, she could not ignore the soldiers and large dogs that stood in front of her. She quickly began to think about what her mother said about acting like a "silly little girl." So she responded to the soldier's questions as she believed her younger sister, Kirsti, would.

Annmarie's courage is a wonderful example of what will be needed to keep as many people as possible out of the harm that is directed at the Jewish people.

As Annmarie was eventually told of the importance of her delivery, she was also told about the courage of others. She learned of the real danger Uncle Henrik faces. She even learns that the deaths of Lise and Peter were not accidents.

Annemarie's special delivery provided an important lesson she will never forget.

Name(s): ______________________________ Date: ____________

______________________________

# Scoring Rubric

Title of novel: ______________________________

| Criteria | Possible Number of Points | Score |
|---|---|---|
| Article addresses an important event or series of events from the novel | 10 | |
| Article sticks to the topic throughout | 10 | |
| Article looks like it came from a newspaper | 10 | |
| Article is interesting and informative | 10 | |
| Article includes accurate information and relevant examples from the novel | 10 | |
| Article is well organized, flows smoothly, and easy to follow | 10 | |
| Article includes relevant quotes from characters | 10 | |
| Article is neat and easy to read | 10 | |
| Article has few spelling, capitalization, and punctuation errors | 10 | |
| Article has few grammatical errors | 10 | |
| **Total Points** | 100 | |

**Teacher's Comments:**

# Mock Trial

What does the activity assess?

- Language Arts Objectives
  - ❑ Understand appropriate verbal/nonverbal techniques for oral presentations
  - ❑ Understand elements of persuasion in spoken texts
  - ❑ Understand character development
- Multiple Intelligences
  - ❑ Linguistic
  - ❑ Interpersonal

What is the assessment activity?

Ask each member of the class to be one of the characters in the novel. The following assignments must be made: judge and defense, and prosecuting attorneys. Depending on the case and class size, the teacher may also want to assign jury duty to several students. You may wish to have a random drawing for character assignments. Tell students their character assignments several days before the mock trial so that they can prepare ahead of time.

Encourage students to dress the part of their assigned characters. Students should know everything their character in the story knows about the plot of the novel that is relevant to the actual court case. They must pretend they do not know the information that was not revealed to their particular character in the course of the novel. Remind students that they should speak from the point of view of their assigned characters.

You may wish to play the part of a bailiff to help monitor and facilitate the trial. The trial that the students present can be a different version of the trial than the one that took place in the novel. The new trial can be based on the premise that all of the facts were not presented in the novel's trial or that a particular character did not receive a fair trial.

What do students need to complete the assessment activity?

- Student Assignment Sheet (page 51)
- Student Planning Sheet (page 52)
- Sample Assessment (page 53)
- Scoring Rubric (page 54)
- Podium for the judge
- Gavel for the judge
- Chairs for the courtroom

How do I grade the assessment activity?

Evaluate each student's ability to participate in a mock trial using the Scoring Rubric (page 54).

 

Name: ______________________________ Date: ______________

# Student Assignment Sheet



The mock trial will be your final assessment of the novel entitled

______________________________________________________________.

Use the Student Planning Sheet and the Sample Assessment to help you prepare for the mock trial.

Please read and follow the guidelines below very carefully. On the day of the trial, you will be expected to:

- Have completed your reading of the novel named above
- Have full knowledge of the plot, setting, and characters described in the novel
- Have prepared for the role that you will play during the trial. Examples: Attorneys should have a list of questions to ask and points to make. Witnesses should have testimony about events.
- Wear a costume that represents your character's role in the novel and trial
- Remain "in character" for the duration of the trial
- Listen to the testimony given during the trial
- Draw conclusions/reach a verdict based on information presented in the trial

Your grade will be based on the Scoring Rubric. Please take time to review the rubric before participating in the mock trial.

Name: ______________________________ Date: ______________

# Student Planning Sheet

**Sample Trial Procedures**

1. Teacher/Bailiff
   - Opens the court proceedings
   - Swears in the witnesses
2. Opening Statements
   - Defense Attorney: introduces himself/herself; summarizes the evidence that will be presented
   - Prosecuting Attorney: introduces himself/herself; explains what the evidence is and what he or she will try to prove using that evidence
3. Direct Examination By the Defense Attorney
   - The defense attorney conducts direct examination (questioning) of all of its own witnesses. At this time, testimony and other evidence is presented. Use this time to develop the facts in support of the case.
4. Cross-Examination By the Prosecuting Attorney
   - The prosecution works to clarify or cast doubt upon the testimony of opposing witnesses. This attorney should point out inconsistencies, bias, and other damaging facts.
5. Direct Examination By the Prosecuting Attorney
   - The prosecution follows the same process as the direct examination by the defense attorney.
6. Cross-Examination By the Defense Attorney
   - The defense follows the same process as the cross-examination by the prosecuter.
7. Closing Arguments
   - Defense Attorney: A closing argument by the defense is a review and analysis of the evidence presented, while indicating how the evidence does not satisfy the elements of the charge against the defendant (accused). Stress the facts that are favorable to your case.
   - Prosecuting Attorney: A closing argument for the prosecution is essentially the same as the defense, except that it argues that the defendant (accused) is guilty based on the evidence presented during the trial.

 

# Sample Assessment

(Excerpt from a trial dialogue based on *The Outsiders*)

**Note:** At the end of *The Outsiders*, Ponyboy said the trial was not what he expected. The following dialogue recreates the trial so that it better meets Ponyboy's expectations.

**Defense Attorney:** Darry, you are Ponyboy's primary caregiver. Is that correct?

**Darry:** Yes, I work two jobs to support him and my other brother, Sodapop.

**Defense Attorney:** If this is true, how did Ponyboy end up in this situation? Why is he here today on trial for murder?

**Darry:** I am very strict with Ponyboy because he is smart; he can be somebody. I want him to be disciplined and follow the rules. At the same time, this is hard because he is surrounded by boys that don't follow the rules. Ponyboy is still learning how to understand why I am so hard on him. All of this happened because he didn't like my rules.

**Defense Attorney:** Do you think an adult could provide Ponyboy with better rules?

**Darry:** No, any kid will try to go against anyone's rules; it's a part of growing up.

**Defense Attorney:** Thanks, Darry. You may step down now. I call Jerry Wood to the stand. Please state your name for the record.

**Jerry Wood:** Jerry Wood.

**Defense Attorney:** How do you know the defendant?

**Jerry Wood:** I am a teacher at his school.

**Defense Attorney:** What kind of student is he?

**Jerry Wood:** Overall, Ponyboy is a good kid. As his brother said, he is trying to find a balance between what he is and what surrounds him. I believe the fact that he risked his life in the fire shows that the real Ponyboy, the good Ponyboy, has power over the other one.

Name: ______________________ Date: __________

# Scoring Rubric

Title of novel: ______________________

| Criteria | Possible Number of Points | Score |
| --- | --- | --- |
| Class works cooperatively | 10 | |
| Trial includes important facts from the novel and sticks to the topic throughout | 10 | |
| Presentation is realistic and is formatted like a trial | 10 | |
| Presentation is creative, interesting, and meaningful | 10 | |
| Trial includes accurate information and relevant examples from the novel | 10 | |
| Trial arguments/testimony is well organized and easy to follow, unless characterization dictates otherwise | 10 | |
| Both sides of the argument are equally presented | 10 | |
| Characterization is consistent with the novel in both spoken responses and mannerisms for the duration of the trial | 10 | |
| Participant speaks loudly and clearly, unless characterization dictates otherwise | 10 | |
| Verdict is based on information presented in the trial | 10 | |
| **Total Points** | 100 | |

**Teacher's Comments:**

# Theme Quilt

What does the activity assess?

- Language Arts Objectives
  - ❑ Make inferences and draw conclusions about the theme of a novel
  - ❑ Improve reading comprehension
- Multiple Intelligences
  - ❑ Linguistic
  - ❑ Kinesthetic
  - ❑ Interpersonal

What is the assessment activity?

Ask students to choose a theme from the novel. Tell them to identify a specific event from the novel that illustrates their chosen theme. More than one student may select a similar theme as long as a different scene is explored by each student. The purpose is to allow students to explore the part of the novel they viewed as meaningful, while showing an understanding of how the theme fits with the novel's overall message.

Give each student a sheet of construction paper to create one patch for the class quilt. Tell students to use their construction paper to show a specific scene or event from the novel. Use a hole punch to put holes around the edge of each piece of construction paper. Invite students to use yarn to connect the pieces of construction paper to create a quilt. Once the quilt is complete, invite students to present their patch to the class. Remind students to explain why the scene or event depicted is important to the novel.

What do students need to complete the assessment activity?

- Student Assignment Sheet (page 56)
- Student Planning Sheet (page 57)
- Sample Assessment (page 58)
- Scoring Rubric (page 59)
- Construction paper
- Markers
- Hole puncher
- Yarn

How do I grade the assessment activity?

Use the Scoring Rubric (page 59) to evaluate each student's quilt patch, which is a means of identifying and explaining important themes in the novel.

Name ______________________________ Date: ______________

# Student Assignment Sheet

You will create a patch for the class quilt based on a theme in the novel and then present it to the class as your final assessment of the novel entitled ______________________________.

Use the Student Planning Sheet and the Sample Assessment to help you prepare your patch for the quilt.

Please read and follow the guidelines below very carefully. Prior to the day we construct the class quilt, you should:

- Have completed your reading of the novel named above
- Have full knowledge of the important themes within the novel
- Plan what will appear on your patch

You may bring craft paper, markers, and other art supplies to create your patch.

Your grade will be based on the Scoring Rubric. Please take time to review the rubric before creating your patch for the class quilt.

Name: ______________________________ Date: ______________

# Student Planning Sheet



Use the space below to draw a sketch of what your patch for the class quilt will look like.

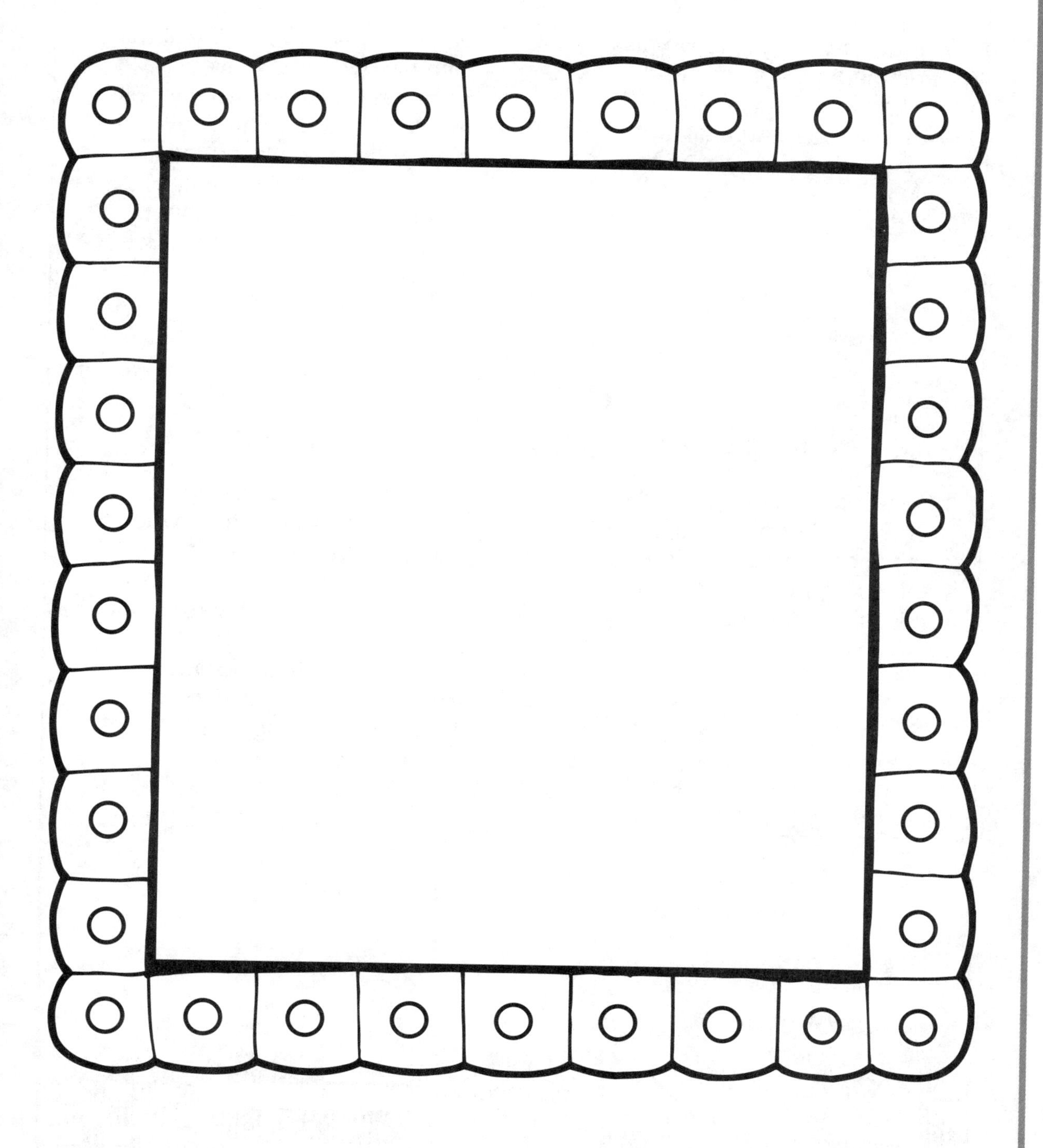

# Sample Assessment

(Theme Quilt Patches based on *The Giver*)

**Bravery**

Jonas is willing to leave his community to enter into the unknown. He does this without receiving his last dosage of bravery from the giver.

**Love**

Jonas is willing to take Gabriel with him when he leaves the community. He knows this will interfere with both his previous plan and his safety, but he loves Gabriel. Once Jonas experiences love, he cannot imagine life without it because he now knows its power.

**Coming of Age**

Jonas comes of age by the end of the book as he experiences many different things. The first indication of this is his stirrings.

**Interdependence**

Throughout the book each child awaits the ceremony to move to the next step in life. This moves the children closer to the ability to survive without their parents. This will also help prepare them for the twelve ceremonies when they begin contributing to the community.

 

Name: ______________________________ Date: ______________

# Scoring Rubric



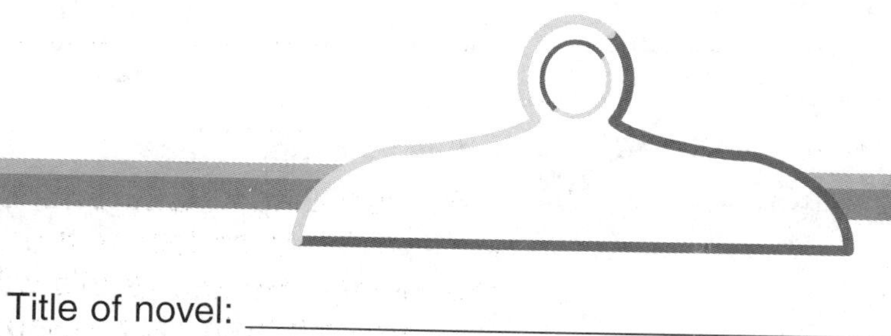

Title of novel: ______________________________

| Criteria | Possible Number of Points | Score |
|---|---|---|
| Patch represents a theme from the novel | 10 | |
| Patch provides details from the novel that support the theme | 10 | |
| Details included on the patch are accurate | 10 | |
| Patch is neat and well thought out with attention to detail | 10 | |
| Patch is creative, interesting, and meaningful | 10 | |
| Student works cooperatively to create the class quilt | 10 | |
| Presentation is an accurate description of a theme from the novel | 10 | |
| Presentation includes an explanation of the theme's relevance to the novel | 10 | |
| Presentation is well organized and easy to follow | 10 | |
| Presentation of information about the patch is loud and clear | 10 | |
| **Total Points** | 100 | |

**Teacher's Comments:**

Obituary

# Obituary

What does the activity assess?

- Language Arts Objectives
  - ❑ Understand implicit statements of attitude and opinion
  - ❑ Reflect on what has been learned from the novel
  - ❑ Analyze setting
  - ❑ Make connections between plot and setting
- Multiple Intelligences
  - ❑ Linguistic

What is the assessment activity?

This assessment allows students to tell the life story of a character from the novel. The character does not have to be deceased. Tell students to create an obituary based on what they know about the character, as well as the predictions they make about the character.

If possible, show students a sample obituary. Discuss the content and format of an obituary to help familiarize students with this type of article.

Tell students to include important information about the life of the character they have chosen. This information should include, but is not limited to, the character's name, date of birth, date of death, age at death, cause of death, parent's names, the names of any surviving relatives, place of residence, and any of the character's accomplishments/achievements.

What do students need to complete the assessment activity?

- Student Assignment Sheet (page 61)
- Student Planning Sheet (page 62)
- Sample Assessment (page 63)
- Scoring Rubric (page 64)
- Sample obituary (optional)

How do I grade the assessment activity?

Evaluate each student's ability to write an informative obituary using the Scoring Rubric (page 64).

Name: ______________________________ Date: ______________

# Student Assignment Sheet

For this assessment, you will pretend to be a writer for the obituary section of the newspaper. You will base your obituary on the life of one of the characters in the novel entitled ______________________________.

The obituary can be for a character that is still living at the end of the book. You can predict information that is not known, such as the character's date and cause of death. Use the Student Planning Sheet and the Sample Assessment to help you write your obituary.

Please read and follow the guidelines below very carefully. The obituary should include the following:

- Name of the character
- Date of birth
- Date of death
- Age at the time of death
- Cause of death
- Education
- Occupation
- Major accomplishments/achievements
- Names of the character's parents
- Names of the character's closest surviving relatives
- Place of residence
- Place of funeral/burial

Your grade will be based on the Scoring Rubric. Please take time to review the rubric before writing the character's obituary.

Name: ______________________________ Date: ______________

# Student Planning Sheet

Before writing the obituary, you will need to gather information about the deceased character. Remember that the obituary can be for a character that is still living at the end of the book. You can predict information that is not known, such as the character's date and cause of death.

| | |
|---|---|
| Name of Deceased | |
| Date of Birth | |
| Date of Death | |
| Age at the Time of Death | |
| Cause of Death | |
| Education | |
| Occupation | |
| Major Accomplishments/Achievements | |
| Names of the Character's Parents | |
| Names of the Character's Closest Surviving Relatives | |
| Place of Residence | |
| Place of Funeral/Burial | |

# Sample Assessment

(Sample Obituaries based on *Wait Till Helen Comes: A Ghost Story*)



## Daily News

VOLUME 1, ISSUE 1
August 9, 1986

## *Obituaries*

### *Helen E. Harper*

*Helen Harper died at the tender age of 7 on August 8, 1886. After escaping the fire at her family home, she attempted unsuccessfully to swim to safety. She drowned as she fought to make it across the pond filled from the previous night's rain.*

*Born to Joseph and Mabel Harper (both deceased) on March 7, 1879, Helen has no surviving relatives.*

*Helen lived a very short and mysterious life. Many community members knew Helen as the little girl that played alone in the pond. Although Helen kept to herself, she will be missed by many members of our community.*

*A small joint memorial service will be held at the church across from the remains of the Harper House. The ceremony will honor Helen, her mother, and her stepfather, Robert Miller.*

*Following the ceremony, Helen will be buried under the oak tree behind the church.*

### *Molly*

*Molly died at the tender age of 12 on August 15, 1986. After returning home following what appeared to be a break in, Molly fell and suffered serious injuries. She fell as she began to run away from the family home in fear that a burglar may have still been in her house. Molly's fall left her with a concussion. She went into a coma from which she never recovered.*

*Molly is survived by her mother, Jean; her brother, Michael; her stepfather, Dave; and her stepsister, Heather.*

*Molly lived a very short but fulfilling life. Many community members knew Molly as the girl who could be found reading Watership Down outside or playing in the woods with her stepsister. Molly will be missed by both her family and the members of our community.*

*A small memorial service will be held at the church sanctuary that was adjoined to Molly's home. Following the ceremony, the family will return to their hometown to bury Molly.*

Name: ______________________ Date: ____________

# Scoring Rubric

Title of novel: ______________________

| Criteria | Possible Number of Points | Score |
|---|---|---|
| Obituary is about a specific character from the novel | 30 | |
| Obituary includes important information about the character's life and death<br>• Date of birth<br>• Date of death<br>• Age at the time of death<br>• Cause of death<br>• Education<br>• Occupation<br>• Major accomplishments and/or achievements<br>• Names of the character's parents<br>• Names of the character's closest surviving relatives<br>• Places of residence<br>• Place of funeral/burial | 30 | |
| Obituary includes accurate information or logical predictions based on the text of the story | 20 | |
| Tone of the obituary is appropriate | 5 | |
| Obituary is neat and easy to read | 5 | |
| Obituary does not include irrelevant information or information about other characters | 10 | |
| **Total Points** | 100 | |

**Teacher's Comments:**

 

# Children's Book

What does the activity assess?

- Language Arts Objectives
  - ❑ Reflect on what has been read
  - ❑ Formulate ideas, opinions, and personal responses to texts
  - ❑ Understand elements of character development
- Multiple Intelligences
  - ❑ Linguistic

What is the assessment activity?

This assessment involves having students write a modified version of the novel they have studied. Ask students to decide which events are the most important in understanding the plot of the story. Tell them to use these events to create a children's version of the novel.

Explain to students that their version of the novel should include dialogue and illustrations that would be appealing to young children. Remind students that the vocabulary and sentences should be appropriate for young readers. Point out that they are telling the plot of the novel in a simple but interesting way.

Encourage students to work cooperatively with a group to complete this assessment.

What do students need to complete the assessment activity?

- Student Assignment Sheet (page 66)
- Student Planning Sheet (page 67); two copies per student
- Sample Assessment (page 68)
- Scoring Rubric (page 69)
- Notebook paper

How do I grade the assessment activity?

Use the Scoring Rubric (page 69) to evaluate students' abilities to write a children's book based on the novel.

Name(s): ______________________________ Date: ______________

______________________________

# Student Assignment Sheet

Your final assessment is to create an illustrated children's book based on the novel entitled ______________________________

Use the Student Planning Sheet and the Sample Assessment to help you write your children's book.

Please read and follow the guidelines below very carefully. Your children's book should include:

- A minimum of ten pages
- An original and creative title
- An interesting retelling of the important events from the novel
- The main characters from the novel
- Simple and easy-to-understand vocabulary and sentences
- Attractive illustrations

Your grade will be based on the Scoring Rubric. Please take time to review the rubric before writing your children's book.

Name(s): ______________________________ Date: ______________

______________________________

# Student Planning Sheet

Work with your group to record information about the most important events from the novel. Then use this information to write your children's book. Be sure to include dialogue and illustrations when you write your book.

Title of novel: ______________________________

| Event | Main Characters | Setting |
|---|---|---|
| | | |
| | | |
| | | |
| | | |
| | | |
| | | |
| | | |
| | | |
| | | |
| | | |

# Sample Assessment

(Excerpt of children's book based on *The Cay*)

**The Cay:**
**Phillip's Blind Adventure**

"I am drowning!" This is the first thought that entered my head. All I could see was water.

Hello, my name is Phillip. This is my adventure story. Read closely. You just might learn something.

1

In case you are wondering, I was saved from the water.

Timothy is a black man. This is important because all my life I was taught to think less of black people. I was told they were different from me. So, any time I came close to him, I backed away.

Blackness surrounds me because I am blind. I hurt my head. The pain went away, but it left me blind. Timothy tries to make me feel better by saying it will go away, but it doesn't. I have to depend on him for everything. I am scared.

2

Timothy gets food from the sea for us. He also builds a shelter for us. I am confused. Are black people really different?

Timothy teaches me how to live with my blindness. I am learning so much.

Then, one day, there is a bad storm. It rips our clothes to shreds. Because Timothy protects me from the storm, it takes away all his energy.

3

Timothy dies. The storm has taken his life away. He is gone. I bury him. I feel scared again.

Timothy taught me how to build a fire to signal for help.

One day a plane flies over, so I signal for help. They come and get me. They do not believe my story about Timothy.

After I was rescued, I had surgery for my eyes. Now I can see again!

This was my blind adventure.

4

Name(s): ______________________________ Date: ______________

______________________________

# Scoring Rubric

Children's Book

Title of novel: ______________________________

| Criteria | Possible Number of Points | Score |
|---|---|---|
| Book includes a minimum of ten pages | 10 | |
| Book has an original and creative title | 10 | |
| Book has an interesting retelling of the important events from the novel | 10 | |
| Book is well organized and events follow the same sequence as the novel | 10 | |
| Book includes main characters from the novel | 10 | |
| Book is creative, interesting, and age-appropriate | 10 | |
| Book has easy-to-understand vocabulary and sentences | 10 | |
| Book includes attractive illustrations | 10 | |
| Book is neat and easy to read | 10 | |
| Book has few spelling, capitalization, grammatical, and punctuation errors | 10 | |
| **Total Points** | 100 | |

**Teacher's Comments:**

# Advertisement

What does the activity assess?

- Language Arts Objectives
  - ❑ Understand elements of character development
  - ❑ Understand inferred and recurring themes in literary works
- Multiple Intelligences
  - ❑ Linguistic

What is the assessment activity?

This assessment allows students to use their creativity to advertise a novel. Explain to students that the purpose of the advertisement is to stress the good points of the novel using what they learned from reading the book. Students can either do a television commercial or printed advertisement. Students can choose to either complete this assessment individually or with a group. Groups may wish to take the assignment further than a single advertisement by doing a more in-depth promotion of the book.

Students should use the advertisement to persuade people to read the novel. They should do this by incorporating quotes from real or imaginary critics and individuals who have read the novel. They should also mention any awards the author has won for writing the book. Tell students to include a brief summary that will encourage people to read the novel.

What do students need to complete the assessment activity?

- Student Assignment Sheet (page 71)
- Sample Assessment (pages 72 and 73)
- Scoring Rubric (page 74)
- Poster board
- Markers, crayons, or paint

How do I grade the assessment activity?

Evaluate students' abilities to create an advertisement for the novel using the Scoring Rubric (page 74).

 

Name(s): ______________________________ Date: ______________

______________________________



# Student Assignment Sheet

You will create an advertisement for the novel as your final assessment of the novel. Your advertisement can be either in the form of a print advertisement that you may see in a newspaper or magazine or in the format of a television commercial/promotion. You are expected to create an original advertisement that will help persuade people who have never read to buy the novel. You may complete this assessment individually or with a group. Use the Student Planning Sheet and the Sample Assessment to help you prepare your advertisement.

Please read and follow the guidelines below very carefully. Your advertisement should include:

- A minimum of five reasons to read the novel
- The author's name
- Quotes from real or imaginary critics
- Quotes from real or imaginary people who have read the novel
- A brief, but interesting, summary of novel
- Awards the author has earned for writing this novel
- An effective use of persuasive techniques

Your grade will be based on the Scoring Rubric. Please take time to review the rubric before completing your advertisement.

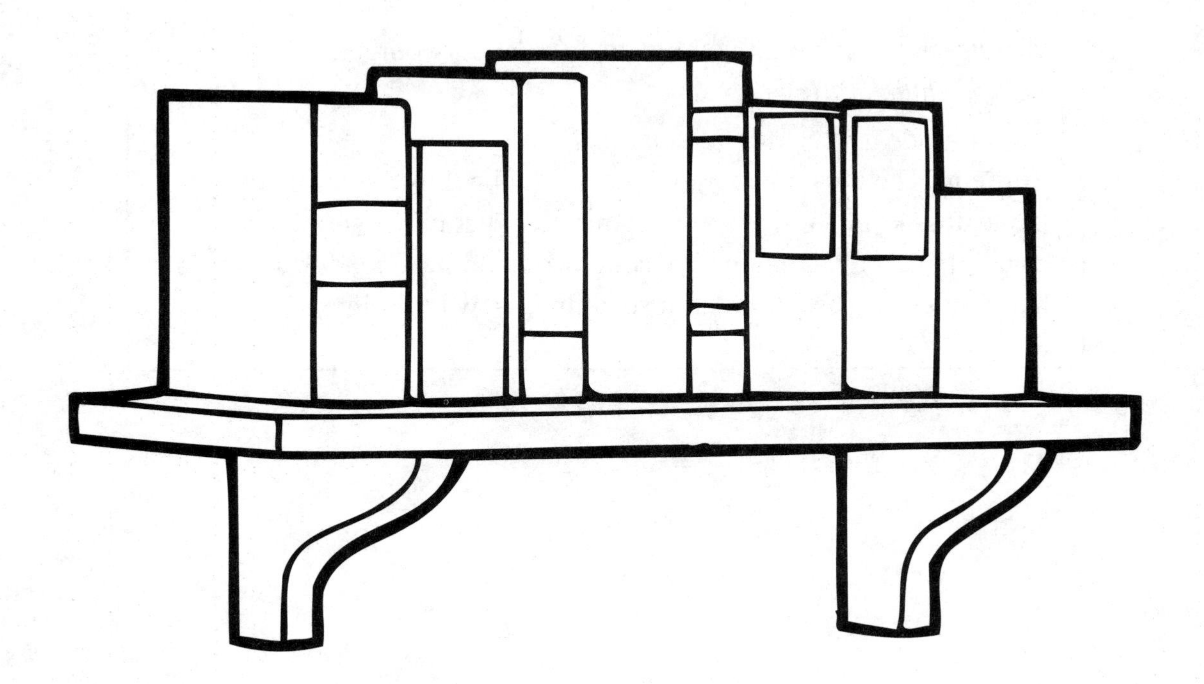

# Sample Assessment

(Excerpt from a promotion based on *Roll of Thunder, Hear My Cry*)

**Note:** Students did a group video promotion for a television advertisement. Students videotaped the scenes in a local library. One group member took on the role of the reporter, attempting to persuade television viewers to read *Roll of Thunder, Hear My Cry*. The other group members played the role of children and adults that had read and enjoyed the novel. Students also made posters advertising *Roll of Thunder, Hear My Cry* that they displayed in the background during the interviews. See the reduced example on page 73.

**Sample Interview #1**

**Reporter:** So, you too have taken part in the current craze to read *Roll of Thunder, Hear My Cry* by Mildred Taylor. Tell us what you think about the novel.

**University Student:** This is not a simple craze. This book will be read for many decades to come. It will become one of the recommended and required classics. It is just wonderful! I loved every word. It has won numerous awards.

**Sample Interview #2**

**Reporter:** What would you like to share about your experience with *Roll of Thunder, Hear My Cry*?

**Student:** The most memorable part of the book is the front cover of the textbook. It showed me how injustice that many viewed as little or unimportant had a huge impact on some. I have read this book a half a dozen times, and I learn something new each time.

 

# *Roll of Thunder, Hear My Cry*

**By Mildred D. Taylor**

**Winner of the 1977 John Newbery Medal**

**A Family Working Together Against All Odds**

Don't miss the opportunity to read this novel!

It is available in bookstores.

# A Must Read !!!

Name(s): ______________________________ Date: ______________

______________________________

# Scoring Rubric

Title of novel: ______________________________

| Criteria | Possible Number of Points | Score |
|---|---|---|
| Information about the novel is presented as a printed advertisement or television commercial/promotion | 10 | |
| Advertisement includes at least five reasons to read the novel | 10 | |
| Advertisement includes accurate information about the novel and author | 10 | |
| Advertisement includes the author's name | 5 | |
| Advertisement is creative, interesting, and well organized | 15 | |
| Advertisement uses quotes from real or imaginary critics | 5 | |
| Advertisement uses quotes from real or imaginary people who have read the novel | 5 | |
| Advertisement includes a brief, but interesting, summary of novel | 15 | |
| Advertisement names awards the author has earned for writing this novel | 10 | |
| Advertisement shows an effective use of persuasive techniques | 15 | |
| **Total Points** | 100 | |

**Teacher's Comments:** ______________________________

 

# Mock Writer's Style

What does the activity assess?

- Language Arts Objectives
  - ❑ Understand specific devices an author uses to accomplish his/her purpose
  - ❑ Understand how language is used to convey mood, images, and meaning
  - ❑ Establish and adjust purposes for reading
  - ❑ Understand how the author's style affects the reader
- Multiple Intelligences
  - ❑ Linguistic

What is the assessment activity?

This assessment allows students to emulate the writing style of an author, as well as to make a personal connection to the subject of the novel. Additionally, students will have the opportunity to explore a type of writing they have not previously experienced.

Ask students to identify what the writer's strengths are, noting the devices and style that makes the writing in the book effective. Have students develop an original piece of writing modeled after the author's work.

Encourage students to focus their writing on a personal experience. Remind them that the experience they write about should have some kind of connection to the content of the novel.

What do the students need to complete the assessment activity?

- Student Assignment Sheet (page 76)
- Sample Assessment Sheet (page 77)
- Scoring Rubric (page 78)

How do I grade the assessment activity?

Evaluate each student's ability to recreate the author's writing style using the Scoring Rubric (page 78).

Name: ______________________________ Date: ______________

# Student Assignment Sheet

Your final assessment will be an original story based on the author's style of writing found in the novel entitled ______________________________.

Use the Sample Assessment to help you write your story.

Please read and follow the guidelines below very carefully. Your story should show that you:

- Have identified the elements that make the novel an effective piece of writing
- Are able to pattern your writing after the author's technique and style
- Have made a meaningful personal connection to the novel

Your grade will be based on the Scoring Rubric. Please take time to review the rubric before writing your original story based on the author's style.

# Sample Assessment

(Sample Mock Writer's Style based on *The House on Mango Street*)

**Roach**

The school bus stopped like it did every day as it arrived in our fallen and destitute neighborhood. I watched Roach get off the bus. Seconds followed, then I saw her hit the other girl, who to me is still nameless. There is another fight. Fights in this neighborhood are part of the environment—a hobby for girls like Roach. Roach's father calls from the corner that if she does not win she will receive a whipping from him, so she fights with all her strength. I don't know what to think.

Another day I sit next to Roach on the school bus. She smiles. Her smile is pretty. I notice one deep dimple in her left cheek. I ask her why she only has one. She tells me someone stole the other one in a fight and never gave it back. We both laugh.

I learned that Roach's real name is Rochelle, but the neighborhood and her father will not let her go by Rochelle right now—maybe some day.

Name: ______________________ Date: ______________

# Scoring Rubric

Title of novel: ______________________

| Criteria | Possible Number of Points | Score |
|---|---|---|
| Story shows that the style and technique used by novel's author has been correctly identified | 20 | |
| Story is based on a personal experience that is connected to the content of the novel | 10 | |
| Story accurately recreates the style and technique used by the novel's author | 20 | |
| Story is creative, interesting, and meaningful | 10 | |
| Story is well organized and easy to follow | 10 | |
| Story is neat and easy to read | 10 | |
| Story has few spelling, capitalization, and punctuation errors | 10 | |
| Story has few grammatical errors | 10 | |
| **Total Points** | 100 | |

**Teacher's Comments:**

# Scoring Rubric

Use the following template to create your own rubric.

Name: ______________________________ Date: ________________

Title of novel: ______________________________

| Criteria | Possible Number of Points | Score |
|---|---|---|
| | | |
| | | |
| | | |
| | | |
| | | |
| | | |
| | | |
| | | |
| | | |

| **Total Points** | 100 | |
|---|---|---|

**Teacher's Comments:**

# Bibliography

This list includes information about the sample novels used in *Novel Assessments for Novels*. Additional titles of books that would be good for these assessments have also been suggested below.


Aiken, Joan. *Wolves of Willoughby Chase*. Bantam Doubleday Dell Books for Young Readers, 1981.

Avi. *Barn*. HarperCollins Children's Books, 1996.

Babbitt, Natalie. *Tuck Everlasting*. Holtzbrinck Publishers, 2000.

Chambers, Veronica. *Marisol and Magdalena*. Hyperion Books for Children, 2001.

Cisneros, Sandra. *The House on Mango Street*. Knopf Publishing Group, 1991.

Cormier, Robert. *The Chocolate War*. Bantam Doubleday Dell Publishing Group, Inc., 1974.

Curtis, Christopher Paul. *The Watsons Go to Birmingham—1963*. Dell Laurel-Leaf, 1995.

Gantos, Jerry. *Joey Pigza Swallowed the Key*. HarperCollins Children's Books, 2000.

Hahn, Mary Downing. *Wait Till Helen Comes: A Ghost Story*. Morrow, William & Co., 1987.

Harper, Lee. *To Kill a Mockingbird*. Warner Books, 1982.

Hinton, S.E. *The Outsiders*. Viking Penguin, 1987.

Lowry, Lois. *The Giver*. Bantam Doubleday Dell Books for Young Readers, 1993.

Lowry, Lois. *Number the Stars*. Bantam Doubleday Dell Books for Young Readers, 1990.

Myers, Walter Dean. *Somewhere in the Darkness*. Scholastic Inc., 1992.

Park, Barbara. *Mick Harte Was Here*. Knopf Publishing Group, 1996.

Paterson, Katherine. *Bridge to Terabithia*. HarperCollins Children's Books, 1987.

Slote, Alfred. *Hang Tough, Paul Mather*. HarperCollins Children's Books, 1995.

Spinelli, Jerry. *Crash*. Random House, 1997.

Taylor, Mildred D. *Roll of Thunder, Hear My Cry*. Puffin, 1991.

Taylor, Theodore. *The Cay*. Avon Books, 1970.

Yolen, Jane. *Wizard's Hall*. Harcourt Brace & Company, 1999.